CW00701147

INSTAGRAM MARKETING SECRETS

FROM ZERO TO ONE HUNDRED THOUSAND FOLLOWERS.

PRACTICAL AND QUICK GUIDE WITH STRATEGIES AND

TECHNIQUES TO BECOME A "REAL" INFLUENCER AND

GET NOTICED ON INSTAGRAM

Harrison H. Philips

Index

Introduction

If you are looking out on Instagram, this is the right guide for you!

In the pages that make up this book, you will find ideas, reflections, and advice on how to create your own, precise, identifiable, and monetizable space using the social network that currently records the highest growth rate in the world.

You will find tips that I have personally tested but, since it is a quick guide and not the encyclopedic, some topics will necessarily be simplified.

I will often tell you about followers, about profiles that have millions of followers, assuming that they are real people, really involved, and not fake bought profiles that are absolutely inactive and only useful to make mass while being, in fact, non-existent. (By the way, I remind you that Instagram periodically does the big cleanups and just a few months ago it eliminated millions of fake accounts, plummeting the popularity of many characters who had grown their fanbase in that way.)

With this book I do not want to give you the magic recipe to become yet another 'influencer,' a term that I find rather unpleasant and that often identifies someone who does not share useful content, but only very beautiful photos and that's it.

What I want to help you do with this book is to create your own profile from which to relaunch your message to the world: be it related to your business or your ideas, your skills, or your aspirations. So, let's start from the beginning.

Rule number one: the metric (that is the measure of the people who follow you) is important but it is not everything.

Chapter 1

Why Instagram?

If you are Beyonce, however, you notice it. Otherwise, giving up the amplification potential of your message represented by Instagram is not very wise, and in some cases, it could be ruinous.

What I mean is that if you are John Doe and not Beyonce and you want to make yourself known or make your products (or services) known, Instagram represents an opportunity for you.

Of course, it is not enough to open your page, post a few photos or videos in a haphazard way to achieve success, run out of inventory and get a billion-euro bank account.

In other words, Instagram unfolds in front of you as a blank page: you can decide what and how to fill it. The contents, as always in social networks, are fundamental: there are so many John Doe in the world that if you do not have precise identifiability, you run the risk of getting lost in the pile.

But why Instagram? That is, until yesterday, we fought with Facebook and today Instagram instead?

It's a matter of numbers, as always: to date, Instagram is the social platform that has the greatest growth trend; in June 2016, monthly Instagram users were 500 million. After 6 months, in December, they had already gone to 600. In the following 4 months, another 100 million users were added, bringing the social network to over 700 million active users in April 2017. In September 2017, another 100 million, until the announcement of the billion in June.

Just do the math: do you really want to be the one who isn't there? Do you want to be the one who does not participate in the "global party" of social media that is experiencing the same boom that Facebook did at the end of the last decade?

You can also decide to stay at home, maybe you are a phenomenon (one of the very few in the world who does not need to communicate to make yourself known), but if you are a normal person, with something to say, or to propose, my advice is to put yourself comfortable in an armchair and concentrate on the next pages where I will tell you what, according to my experience and according to that of many other 'influencers,' works and what doesn't. In short, in the next pages, you will find the currently valid rules to be recognizable, position yourself in the best way according to your needs, and start (or continue even more) to make known who you are and what you do, eventually managing to monetize your social presence.

1.1 How Instagram Can Help You

We understand that being there is indispensable but not sufficient.

If you consider that Instagram has a billion users (as of June 2018), likely, the people you want to reach with your message are there as well. Whatever it is.

Do you want to position your brand? Instagram is the place.

Do you want to make your services known? Instagram is the place.

Do you want to make your vegan recipes known? Instagram is the place.

Do you want to gain popularity for your new political party? Instagram is the place.

The moment you open a profile and start producing content (we'll talk later about how to produce it), you can potentially reach a billion-odd people who care what you have to say or show, or sell.

Instagram will help you achieve your goal, but not by magic. It will do this by recognizing and rewarding your content, which you have been able to create to reach exactly, or almost exactly, whoever interests you.

Whatever sector you move into (photography, crafts, make-up, or gardening), on Instagram you have a huge pool of people who are ready to 'look' at what you propose.

You might think, however, that your product or service cannot be offered to the world through Instagram; for example, if you market sports equipment for ninety-year-old marathon runners, you might be led to say: "No, this is not my platform, it is not my place, there aren't ninety-year-old marathoners here."

You might think so, but you'd think badly.

Because among the billion of users on Instagram it is highly probable (I would say more than anything else sure) that there are children, grandchildren, relatives up to 7th grade, neighbors, and caregivers of the sprightly ninety-year-old who, in fact, are there. It means that the communication does not need to follow a straight line to work.

Even the grandmothers of teenagers who don't even know what Instagram is, know who Kim Kardashian is.

I understand that it is not easy to be Kim Kardashian, but the principle that she embodies is evident.

Instagram can be the amplifier of your message even if it does not reach directly the people you are addressing it to, but to someone who is close to them and who, scrolling the timeline, comes across your photo or video.

Roughly speaking: if you know the rules of Instagram and learn to use them strategically for your purpose, it makes you sell; yourself, your brand, or your ideas.

It helps you to get out of anonymity; it spreads what you are and what you do in the same way as the pebble is thrown into the pond.

What is sure is that the first step you have to take is to understand which pebble you are, that is, to sit down somewhere and honestly answer these three questions:

1. Who am I?
2. What are my goals?
3. Who are my ideal clients?

1.2 Which Are My Goals

Here, let's start with the fundamentals.

Where did you sit down to ask yourself this question?

Are you sitting on a train, on a plane bound for Fantasyland, or are you comfortable on the sofa with a blanket and the cat on your lap?

The first step, the one on which the strategy you plan depends, is the following: you have to understand who you are and what you really want.

If your goal in life is to brush the cat and you want to reach all the serial cat brushers on the planet to become their point of reference (because nobody brushes cats the way you brush Puppy) without ever moving from your sofa, Instagram can help you.

The same: if you're a globe-trotter sleeping in the Borneo Forest and playing chess with lions in Namibia, Instagram can help you become the go-to point of all extreme travelers in the world.

But you have to decide who to reach based on who you really are (don't cheat yourself, if you are a brusher, do not try to be Indiana Jones, because the only result you would achieve is a photo of yourself with a poster of palm trees behind and the cat's tail that you forgot to retouch).

On social networks, the fiction does not work, or in any case, you will be caught soon.

The filters that flatten wrinkles and features can alter the image you give of yourself, but not your true nature and that, inevitably, in the end, will prevail because no home brusher would resist in life as a globe-trotter, and the same the opposite is true.

Understanding who you are and what your communication goals are will help you develop a strategy that can enhance your strengths.

So be honest and choose how to position yourself based on your identity.

I'll give you an example:

If you are a beautician and want to make your salon known, the products you sell, and the formidable anti-cellulite technologies you use, it will be completely useless for your purpose to publish videos in which you comment on the geopolitical situation in Libya. Maybe you also have very sensible things to say about it, but they will hardly be functional in making you reach the goal you have set: making your salon known (unless, because exceptions are always possible, you do not want to take care only of cellulite and wrinkles of geopolitics experts who, coming to you will find a counterbalance for comparison, as well as two good hands for a treatment).

The next step is to understand who your audience is, that is, those people who may be interested in your message, those willing to buy your product or service, and therefore to provide you with a monetizable return on your Instagram communication strategy.

For example:

If you are a ladies' hairdresser, your message must go to women. If you specialize in asymmetrical cuts, even assuming more and more grannies are getting purple hair with blue undertones, your clients are much more likely to be young.

And so far, we have identified two categories: women and young people, therefore, under 50.

If your shop is in Houston, then, it will be important that your follower target is identified in a pre-established geographical area (in jargon we speak of geolocation) within a radius of about fifty kilometers: it will be very difficult for a twenty-three-year-old from Los Angeles to come to you to get her hair done!

In short: before leaving, when you have clarified who you are and what you want to get from Instagram, also try to understand who you want to talk to, who you want to capture attention.

To sum it up: clarify who you are, define your goal, find your audience, and start working (because yes, if you want Instagram to help you get to know you and what you do, you need to know that you have to be willing to invest: in economic terms and time).

1.3 How Much You Are Willing to Invest (Money and Time)

That is: it always costs you less than being blown away by the competition.

Making yourself known through social media is not a game: it is a rather serious matter that requires time and, of course, money.

All the 'influencers' who are on Instagram, and I'm not talking about those who have a following of 1000 people, but those who have tens of thousands, are organized and, above all, have understood that they must produce quality content and with a certain frequency to be known.

One of the most striking examples that comes to mind is that of Marques Brownlee.

Marques reviews the world of technology.

Except that he is not the new guy, but he is someone who has started using social media and the web to make himself known and position himself and, to date, he has almost 3mil. followers on Instagram, plus all the others on other platforms.

He started with YouTube videos that hardly anyone watched at first, but he didn't give up. He invested his time, even before his economic resources, to continue to produce content of value, that is, that was useful for his audience, which contained an immediately usable message.

He has made a thousand tests and attempts to understand what his niche was, the one from which to progressively enlarge his audience.

From YouTube, he switched to Facebook, following the trend

of the social market at a time when Zuckerberg's platform was so popular and now he produces daily video content on Instagram and Instagram TV.

You may think that what he did, or what I did, or hundreds of other people who have learned to use social media to make themselves known or to sell their products and services, is too difficult to replicate.

Well, man, it isn't.

It is a matter of deciding, once again, how much you are willing to invest. How much time per day, week, and month are you ready to devote to growing your personal profile? Translated, how much time are you ready to dedicate to creating valuable content for the people who follow you, or who will follow you?

If you are not willing to spend your time and energy on this purpose, if you do not want to work on your project to make it a winning project, using all the potential that Instagram puts at your service, then it will be very difficult for you to obtain useful results, that is, monetizable.

Don't you have enough time to produce some valuable material to share on Instagram?

Assuming that you want to do it, and not at an amateur level, you can also entrust your message to a team of people who have the necessary expertise to do, in your place, the daily 'dirty work' of production and sharing. It has a cost, but less than being swept away by the competition, right?

On the other hand, if you don't want to invest even a little money to make your content visible to an audience that is genuinely interested in what you propose, hashtags and tags will not be enough to make you known.

Instagram is, again, a clean platform that has far fewer privacy restrictions than Facebook, but which responds to market logic just like Facebook. Just think that a few months ago, when Zuckerberg launched IGTV, many were ready to bet on an Instagram television flop.

And in fact, things weren't going very well at first, but then Instagram decided to promote its TV and made sure that the uploaded videos had a one-minute preview on the authors' personal profile.

Do the math, the investment in time and money, unsuccessful attempts, and other focused ones, give me satisfaction because Instagram has decided to invest in its new product to make it known to an ever-wider audience, rewarding those who believe in it and use it.

One more thing to take into account: in a first phase, that is, as soon as you look out on Instagram you can take advantage of the organic visibility, that is the spontaneous and natural one, favored by the social algorithm, but then, progressively, this tends to decrease in favor of the paid one, that is the one deriving from your investments to sponsor your content, which is always guaranteed because in the end the law also applies here: money is money!

It's a spinning wheel, that of Instagram, it's up to you to choose whether to go up or stay down.

But if you've made it this far, you're probably thinking this wheel could have a good spin for you too.

1.4 Exercise to Do Right Away

Check list:

- Open your account;
- Start following people who are already your customers;
- Look around, see what your competitors are doing;
- See who their audience is (it must also be yours, or better, just yours!);

- Listen sideways: for example, when you need to identify your audience, you can start asking the people you are in contact with what interests them. Listening sideways means going to the root of their request, beyond words. It means reaching the true desire of each one;
- Start posting content that takes into account the tips we've shared so far: who you are, what you do on Instagram, invest.

Chapter 2
Who Are You Addressing to?

For a message to work, it is not enough that it is effective, that is, able to perform the task for which it was created, it must also be well addressed.

If you, for example, are an expert in nanotechnologies, it will not be enough for you to publish photos and videos in which you tell, or immortalize, the latest discovery in the sector, perhaps choosing to put on a more or less large budget to sponsor these contents; if you don't know exactly the people who will be interested in what you are sharing, this is useless.

The point, therefore, that we are going to analyze in this second chapter is your audience.

Because without it, without those who are willing to listen, see, and share your content, your message deflates like a balloon: maybe what you say is amazing and you know how to say it, but if you say it to the wrong people, it is almost (I say almost because extremes never work, not even in the communication) as if you never did it.

And it would be a great shame: if you have something to say, to propose, to share, or to sell, and if you understand who to say it, propose it, and sell it, your margins of success will grow exponentially.

2.1 Who Exactly Is Your Audience

Each platform has its own specific audience that receives a certain type of message, not necessarily cross-media.

Translated: it is not said that if you do a great job on Facebook, with a certain language and a type of communication, you can be equally good on Instagram, or YouTube.

Each medium you use has its own specific code that works for its audience: this is clearly from the content of the message.

The container is the content, it is a principle that you must take into account when you go in search of your audience.

Since we are talking about Instagram in this guide, then perhaps it is appropriate to understand who, on average, the people who frequent it are.

According to data from blog.hootsuite.com, on Instagram, there are over a billion profiles around the world, of which:

- 51.7% are women, 49.3% are men;
- Only 1% of global users (both men and women) declare they are over 65 years old. The majority of women belong to the 18–24 group (15%) and the 25–35 group (15%). Same thing for men (17% in the 18–24 range, and always 17% in the 25–35 range);
- According to the 2019 Digital Report by Hootsuite and We Are Social, 65% of American internet users use Instagram;
- About 20% of those who see a Story on Instagram then comment on it;
- The time spent watching videos on Instagram increases by 80% every year.

Summing up, we can say that on Instagram there is a heterogeneous audience of young men and women who, if properly involved, will comment and interact with you if you know how to send them a correct message, able to capture their attention. Also, they will be ready to watch your videos, published on IGTV, which they will preview for a minute on your profile.

Who are the people I am addressing?

What interests do they have?

What are their jobs?

Are they people who speak the super technical language and want super technical videos or smarter and more understandable videos?

What age range do I target?

What level of education can they have?

Are they men or women?

What time of day do they connect?

How much time do they have to hear what I have to say?

On a social network rather than another, things change radically, starting with the money factor: the sponsored, the posts and videos on which you invest money to show them to the largest number of people. You pay for them.

If you fail to identify your audience, even if you are sharing the most fantastic content in a story, you will get a disappointing result, you will have wasted time and money and in the end, you may come to think that on Instagram there is not your customer (which instead is there, maybe a little hidden, but in one way or another it is there).

2.2 Is Your Customer on Instagram?

Yes, he is there, look! I don't want to be an absolutist, but 99.9% he is there.

You just have to find him, understand how to capture his attention first, and then propose yourself to him with your message, your product, and your service.

Instagram, as we have now understood, is still a 'clean' social network, a place where it is still possible to open communication channels even with potential customers.

To give you an example:

A few weeks ago, I discovered that there were at least a couple of very important personalities from the Italian industry who had a personal profile with few followers.

I wrote to them and, immediately afterward, they replied because, if perhaps on Facebook the direct message box is always more or less clogged, it is not yet on Instagram, and therefore it is easier to get in touch and exchange content even privately.

Recently, Instagram has introduced a new filter for messages that allows you to first view those sent by the profiles with the highest number of followers.

Keep this in mind in the future (it's clear that if you've just opened your account you won't have many people following you, but we're here to improve that too, aren't we?).

No matter how niche the industry you operate in, what matters is that you can reach the people you care about.

At the beginning of this guide, we talked about the measurement criteria to keep in mind to understand if a profile works or not and we had already mentioned that it is not necessary to have millions of followers to work on Instagram.

Let's say you are an accordion maker and the accordion community in Italy is made up of 24,000 people.

If your Instagram profile is followed by 15 thousand of them, you are killing it because you are positioned very well in your reference niche.

Therefore, the fact to understand is how and where to go to look for your customers, and for this, there are two systems developed by Instagram, which I will talk about in the next paragraph.

2.3 Define Your Buyer Persona (Your Customer)

If you want to expand your business on Instagram (and generally on the web) and identify your ideal customer, you have to start by creating your buyer persona.

The buyer personas are representations, therefore hypotheses, of your 'perfect' buyer.

Being representations, they are based at the same time on concrete data and on hypotheses relating to the demographic characteristics, behaviors, motivations, and objectives that each of them has.

Basically, they are generalizations of who you would like your customers to be, but (be careful) they are not your current customers.

Building one or more buyer persona is easy because it involves identifying, perhaps by interviewing a sample of customers you already have or by acquiring data through Google Analytics and similar tools, a series of more or less common characteristics on which, in a second phase, to calibrate your message.

Below we show you some examples of buyer personas.

In general, to build your ideal buyer persona, take these factors into account, without which your hypothesis runs the risk of being too approximate:

- Biographical and demographic data (for example woman, graduated, single, thirty, from East Coast, West Coast);
- Behaviors (sportswoman, art lover, gardening enthusiast, etc.);
- Skills (job, in which field and position);
- Needs (what she is looking for, what she needs).

To create your ideal buyer persona there are many templates that you can easily download and use such as this one:

https://try.alexa.com/offer/ebook/buyer-persona-template

2.4 Exercise to Do Right Away

Now that you understand that your customer is on IG, all you have to do is identify him/her, so take a pen and paper (or turn on your laptop) and outline all the characteristics following these guidelines:

- How old is she/he?
- Is the customer a man or a woman?

- Where is she/he located?

- What interests her/him?

- What kind of work does she/he do?

- What Instagram pages does she/he follow?

- What does she/he publish on IG?

Please note that the more detailed the description of the person you want to reach, the greater the chances you will have of catching her/his attention.

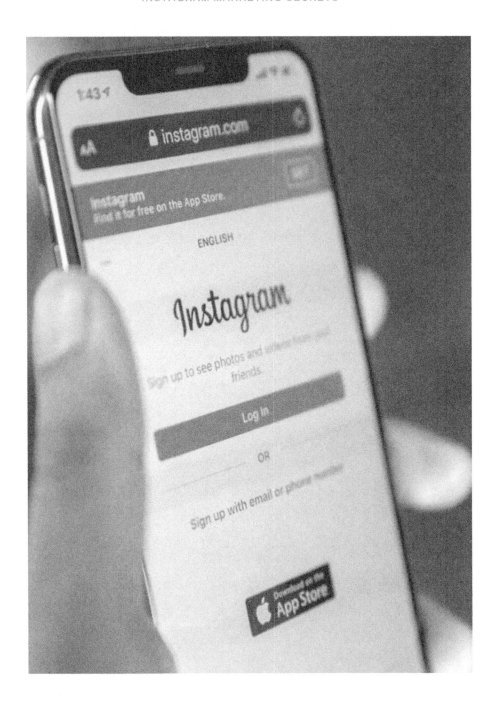

Chapter 3
Create Your New Account

At this point, the premises are all there: you know who you are, the goal you want to achieve, who will be the audience your photos and videos will be directed to and so it's time to start working.

In this chapter, we will see how to build your Instagram account, but not a 'normal' account, an account that rocks, that is, one that reaches exactly the goal you have set.

3.1 Your Name on Instagram

Premise: the name may not be everything, but it is a lot for sure.

The name identifies and, if it is the right one, is engraved in the memory of your followers.

For the choice of the name on your Instagram profile you have these possibilities:

1. if you want to create a personal brand, that is a profile that is linked to you as a person, then you should use

your name (some use only the name, others name, and surname; however, check that the nick you want to use is still available);

2. If you have a company and want to promote your products or services, simply use the name of your brand.

Think of Nike, Gucci, Karl Lagerfeld, Volkswagen, of course, if you are Nike or Volkswagen, you are already a brand, while if you are John Doe, owner of a bathroom furniture shop called "Wet and Happy" the question is a bit different.

On the other hand, the Instagram profile is used to create your brand, to make it known, and identify an ever-growing number of customers, who, given the size of your business, don't need to be 90 million like in Nike's case.

Jeff Bezos, the founder of Amazon, has his own personal profile, from which he relaunches the contents of Amazon, but the Amazon profile is independent of that of Bezos.

3.2 Your Bio (about You)

Having solved the question of the name, Instagram gives you the possibility to define who you are and what you do using the biography: a space in which, by carefully choosing a few words, you present yourself to whoever arrives on your profile.

If you are Leonardo Di Caprio, it is not necessary to write that you are an actor in your bio, everyone knows who you are. However, in general, it is always a good idea, net of Leo Di Caprio and all the famous people who do not need an introduction, to indicate which your industry is.

In mine, I chose to write "Entrepreneur," because it is my job, my main occupation.

Indeed, I'm also a husband, friend, cousin, etc., but the goal of my Instagram profile is to grow my business, not to show around how beautiful my wife is or how nice my friends are.

So, when I had to choose a word that identified me, I chose "Entrepreneur."

If you are John Doe who wants to position himself as a nano particles' expert, then you could write Physicist in your bio and add, if you deem it necessary to reinforce your credibility, other details concerning what you do.

So you could write: Physicist, a researcher at MIT, a teacher at... etc.

Some, such as Michelle Obama, add a passion that distinguishes them from their work and their role within the family (in the case of mother and wife). Michelle is in fact a dog lover too: scrolling her feeds you will find photos in which she is with her family, at work, and also a couple of photos of her dogs.

Keep in mind that if you write that you are a hermit crabs' lover people will expect you to post something about them.

In the biography, you can, and I recommend it, also insert the link to your site, if you have one.

If you are a company, waiting for the experiment conducted in recent months by Instagram to end and start selling your products directly from the social network, inserting the link to your site (or to that of a particular product or service you want to promote in a certain period) could be functional for this purpose, taking into account the fact that you can change and replace the link as many times as you want.

In the same way, if you have your own website, even if you

don't actually sell anything, but offer services or consultancy, the link to your site is a way for people to know you better without having to mess around with Google (that is: closing the app, typing your name on the search tool, and finding your website).

The more you make something simple and immediate, the better chance you have that something will be used, so in your bio, if you have it, don't forget to link your website.

Many characters insert a phrase that represents them, a motto, a slogan, something quick and easy to memorize.

Britney Spears wrote:

Artist, Mamma, Pray Every Day, Chef in the works.

You can choose whether or not to write your slogan or that of your company, perhaps having it followed by an emoticon, but do not overdo it by adding a thousand emoticons or you could risk appearing as a scoundrel, other than the phenomenon of nanoparticles or the most trusted among bathroom accessories sellers.

To Sum Up

Keep these points in mind when creating your Instagram bio:

- Include a brief description of who you are and/or what you do, for example, Lawyer/former swimming champion, journalist, entrepreneur, etc.
- You can also opt for the interests that characterize you or the topics you deal with and start from those, for example, Business, Marketing, Digital;
- Add your contacts (e-mail address and website);
- Use the bio also for the "call to action": you can share a link, which you can change whenever you want;
- In general, remember that there is no single and indisputable rule: therefore, try, experiment, and see what works best for you!

3.3 Your Image

Let's repeat together: "Fiction doesn't work," especially when it comes to choosing your profile picture.

However, if you choose a truly professional photo, it stands out. There is a line that can be seen between an ugly and spontaneous photo and a beautiful, true, and professional one.

So based on how you want to position yourself, you will have a consequent image, but if you can, invest in a professional photo that reflects you.

Until recently it was not like this: between filters and Photoshop, it was all a flourishing of beautiful and flawless faces, sculpted muscles, and six-packs.

They were literally beautiful photos, studied in detail, from the lights to the shots, with refined poses: in other words, photos designed for pleasure.

And I'm not just talking about people, even the places underwent the same treatment: the sea was getting bluer, the hotel rooms, even 2 stars hotels, seemed extra luxurious ones, the houses looked like palaces...but then you bump your nose in the reality that it was of a somewhat shabby hotel, a dimly lit two-room apartment, and a beer belly.

Gradually, therefore, the attempts at extreme and perhaps a bit cheating of the truth have been exposed and have stopped working.

Just to give you an idea, Nike, that colossus with 90 million followers, has recently launched a campaign in which there is a model who appears with unshaved armpits: net of everyone's tastes, what is evident is the return to the most natural, dirtiest, truest photos.

If you consider that live videos that inevitably cannot be artificial and Stories work a lot on Instagram today, we can close the circle concerning this new trend towards naturalness.

Given this first point, I would not like you to think that there is no study or reflection behind the choice of an image which, as we have said, is truer and 'dirty' than in the past but has not changed its own basic goal: to get noticed, capture the attention of those who are scrolling their feed and, possibly, make them remain as a follower to interact with.

What I advise you to do is to be like Nike, of course, according to your possibilities, the audience you want to intercept, and the product or service you want to make known.

The goal is to hit, right from your profile picture, but without deceiving those who look at you or what you are proposing for the first time.

Instagram is still a 'clean' social network that rewards messages and content that meets this criterion. There is an ethic, that of honesty, that works here more than elsewhere.

Your message and your photos must be consistent with who you are and what you do, but in the same way, they must be able to be remembered.

There certainly is something that can characterize you, start looking for it and photograph it to start, right from your profile picture (which goes together with your name and your bio), to tell who you are.

Finally, a piece of advice borrowed from Rory Sutherland:

"The opposite of an excellent idea can be an excellent idea."

By this I mean that there isn't just one way, or one idea, to make your profile work well.

Experimenting irrationally, going in the opposite direction to what everyone is following can be winning, otherwise, you end up confusing yourself with the mass, while you have to find your corner of uniqueness, the one that will allow you to stand out and position yourself in a clear and defined way.

To Sum Up

Keep these tips in mind when choosing your profile picture:

- The photo must reflect your brand and your positioning;
- Choose an evergreen image: do not use a photo that explicitly refers to a particular season, like you at the seaside (because in winter it doesn't work) unless, of course, your brand does not produce swimwear;
- Look at the size of the photo which today is a 110x110 square;
- You can use objects that represent you: if you are a tennis player, for example, you can use a photo with a racket, if you are a cook, you can use a ladle or flour or a chef's hat, etc.

3.4 Exercise to Do Right Away

Have you already had an Instagram profile in which, to date, you have posted photos of holidays, work, kittens, mother-in-law, puppies, shoes, funny selfies, and any other possible nice or cute image that has crossed your mind?

Well, then it's time for a change.

Let's start with the big cleanings (I did them too when I

decided to use my profile well) and proceed by steps:

- Delete, without regret, those photos and videos that are not functional to achieve the purpose you have set for yourself;
- Check that your name corresponds to what you want to communicate, corresponds to you, and is easily memorable;
- Write your new bio using the suggestions you found in this chapter;
- Choose a profile photo that talks about you, that is not fake but is particular enough to intrigue those who see it.

Chapter 4
You Have to Give Content to Your Followers

Now that you have the container, the time has come to fill it with content, which on Instagram means filling it with quality photos and videos, making the most of all the possibilities that this social network offers you.

In fact, it is not very useful to have an Instagram profile if you leave it empty or use it in a non-strategic way concerning your goal, whether it is to position yourself and make yourself known as a shell expert or to sell your product (or service); now is the time to create content that is consistent with the result you want to achieve.

In this chapter, based on my experience and the observation of other profiles that work, I will share with you what I think are the tips that can help you make your Instagram profile a good one now.

4.1 Quantity Makes the Difference

Given that the quality of what you publish is very important (unless the strategy you have chosen is to share only bad photos and videos on your profile...and this is also a strategy and maybe it works) the first aspect not to be forgotten is that on Instagram the quantity pays.

Appearing every day on your followers' feed with a photo, story, or video, causes their attention to inevitably be captured by that guy (or girl, of course) who posts every morning at 9 am something that interests them, who it makes them smile, makes them curious, stimulates them to reflect, etc.

We said right away that a profile that works, that is, that reaches the goal it has set for itself, implies commitment and perseverance by those who create it.

First of all, it is a matter of investing time to produce content, which may not be 'perfect' at the beginning and certainly can be improved, but which will allow you not to be forgotten and to gradually ensure a group of people who are loyal and really interested in you, what you say and what you do.

There are two principles that you shouldn't forget to build a profile that works.

The first is that the constant, daily, or almost daily production of content makes you, in the medium term, a reference point for a certain number of people (who are the ones that really interest you because, in turn, they are interested in what propose to them).

The second is precisely the number of these people: before you get desperate because your profile is not followed by a "zillion" of people, it is good to remember that perhaps the sector in which you operate has a limited audience.

In any case, whether you have a potential audience of 7 billion people or have 700 followers, you have to produce content for them.

You must, or should, do it with a quite high frequency using all the possibilities that Instagram offers you: photos, Stories, and videos (both for the profile and for IGTV).

It is better if you alternate them so that you always offer something new to those who follow you.

4.2 How to Create Daily Content

I know that producing original content, daily, is not a trivial matter.

It takes time and perseverance and some precautions to make the best use of the material that is produced.

If on the one hand with the advent of Stories, Instagram has favored a fast and temporary way of communicating (the Stories you publish disappear after 24 hours), on the other hand, this tool ensures that at any time, wherever you are, you can share your content live with those who follow you.

Publishing Stories (which I will talk about later) is a way to stay in constant contact with the people who follow you, sharing your daily life with them.

Another matter is the videos, both those for Instagram and those for IGTV.

On Instagram TV I dedicate a separate paragraph, so let's come to the original videos for Instagram.

I understand that it is difficult to post daily content, but you can always try to organize yourself, for example by dedicating two hours to recording a long piece of content that you can cut into several clips.

You don't need to have special editing software or super expensive cameras to record: you just need your phone and an app, like InShot, to produce good quality videos. (Remember that the ideal format for IG is square!)

If you organize yourself, perhaps making a list of the topics you want to talk about, it is certainly easier not to lose the thread of the discussion (i.e., start it and finish it without getting lost in digressions) and identify the exact points in which to cut it to get a good number of clips, which I advise you to complete with bands at the top and bottom in which to write the title and, possibly, subtitles.

As for the pictures, we have already said that they must be able to capture the attention and that today those that are too glossy, now seen and overwhelmed, can no longer do it.

So ok to 'dirty' images (I am thinking of those that Chris Hemsworth often posts on his profile, not official photo shoots but his real-life ones), real, true, in which it is easier for your followers to identify themselves.

A text message is always linked to these: a sentence, or a longer caption, which summarizes what that photo represents, and which must always be consistent and uniform with the overall style of the profile.

Each photo or video can also be linked to hashtags (keywords preceded by the # sign), which have the express purpose of allowing better indexing of the content.

Let me explain: hashtags allow you to facilitate the search for posts by topics and to connect people with common interests.

To Sum Up

If you organize and plan your time, you have the opportunity to publish daily original content specifically aimed at the people who follow you. Whether it's a video, a story, a photo, you have many ways to not lose contact with your followers.

4.3 Plan It or Wing It

On Instagram there is space for both types of communication: you can schedule and plan your feeds, or you can, equally, improvise and post them right away.

Let's say that the most suitable tool, perhaps born for this purpose, are the Stories, in which you recover, or resume the context in which you are, resulting in a video of about 15 seconds visible for 24 hours (take into account this Stories 'mortality' thing because it's so useful for experimenting and seeing what works and what doesn't!).

In general, it is good that we do not forget that Instagram was born as an aesthetic portfolio and therefore rewards, by its very nature, beauty, understood here as uniformity of contents.

It is clear, therefore, that beyond the fact that you publish improvising or after a long and careful reflection, you will be better recognized if you have a very specific communication style that makes you unique.

This means that often, even behind an apparent improvisation, there is a careful study of what is shown. We could say that improvisation works best if it is a little thought out unless you are, for example, Jimmy Fallon and therefore you are a phenomenon in improvising in front of a camera.

Having made these premises, you must know that Instagram, like Facebook, also allows you to schedule your posts: in fact, you can publish your content even in subsequent moments to those in which you have prepared them.

Until recently this was not possible, but for a few months, Zuckerberg and associates have decided that even on Instagram you can use post scheduling. But, unlike Facebook, you cannot do it directly from the social network, but you have to use tools (there are several, including Iku Social, Skedsocial, HopperHQ, and Grum) that allow you to schedule videos and photos.

Planning is very useful if, for example, you manage a company profile because it allows you to upload, at the same time, more posts that will then be published in the days and times you have established (perhaps considering the moments when those who follow you are more present on social networks and more willing to interact with you).

Once uploaded, the only thing you will have to take care of is to monitor its progress, reply to comments and direct messages (DMs).

A nice step forward for social media managers who manage multiple profiles for work, but a small revolution also for those who have decided to use their own in a 'professional' way and who now have the possibility of using programming tools to publish content at the right moment.

I'll give you an example:

You are a dog expert and you know that in three weeks there will be the largest gathering of dog owners in the world. That week you won't be able to publish anything for many reasons but no problem, you can use the programming tools to load your content in which you illustrate uses and customs of all known and unknown dog species in the world.

Programming leaves you free time to think about the next content; improvising allows you, perhaps, to be more direct, but if you are just starting out on Instagram, a little planning could help.

However, keep in mind that Instagram could soon remove the ability to schedule posts and return to being a 'live' social network.

4.4 Which Content Is Right for You

Not everything is good for everyone, this is true in general, and also applies to Instagram. There are in fact several variables to consider starting with your character and personality.

If you are shy and introverted, maybe the Stories don't really suit you (at least at the beginning). But if you are confident in front of the camera, the Stories are just perfect for you.

Whatever you are, whatever your temperament, Instagram

can be useful to you.

Because even the most pathological shy person can start producing videos to promote his products or services.

As always, it's a matter of training: my first videos are not comparable to those of today.

Over the years I have tried, experimented, looked for different solutions, asked for advice, and looked at what others were doing.

I made mistakes and tried not to forget them.

Once you understand it, once you have made your mistakes (as Americans say: "get it wrong quickly!"), then you have found your strategy, the one perfectly tailored to you.

And then you can move on to the next step, which is to understand if that strategy is also suitable for the product or service you want to promote.

If you have the natural joy of Mozart while composing the Requiem and you need to make known your company that produces carnival jokes, it may not be immediate for you to appear on video with that vital charge to talk about how funny your jokes are (unless, and anything can happen in the fabulous world of social media, you are so good at the subtle art of paradox and, dressed as a Death Eater, can convey the right message).

I believe that everything can be promoted and made known on Instagram; once again it is a question of deciding what is fairer, what works best starting from the basics that I have shared with you in this guide.

The way you have to understand this is to proceed by attempts, error, and second thoughts until the results arrive.

If you do it, if you insist and do not give up when they are late in arriving if you understand who you should contact and how you should do it (while continuing to monitor the progress of your posts, your videos, and your Stories), of course, you will come to understand what your perfect content is, what works best and from there on you can really start getting the results you aspire to.

4.5 Videos on Instagram and IGTV

The point is not to be caught unprepared: it is not necessary to be a "precocious user," as long as you keep your eyes open on the social world and know how to grasp its daily revolutions.

Instagram has always given the possibility to post videos on your profile, clips that can be used, as we have seen, to promote yourself or your products.

The 'classic' videos for the Instagram profile have a 1:1 format, that is, the so-called 'square,' or bundled, with the bands at the top and bottom, preferably with writings explaining the crucial steps, they are a very useful tool.

They could be of any type, based on the message you want to share with the people who follow you: it could be you talking and explaining something, you commenting with someone on a news story, they could be videos of your product, etc.

They could be nice or very serious (the former usually works better, but nothing prevents you from trying how the latter works, maybe you are a phenomenon and only go great when serious).

Think of Adrian Fartade, a science writer who has made astronomy fun and accessible (his Instagram profile has 35,000 followers, Facebook has 95,000, and his YouTube channel has 182,000 subscribers).

He is nice, genuine, and makes something complicated

understandable in a different way than his colleagues.

Adrian, whom I follow, has become a character, in his own area, precisely because he has been able to use his ability to simplify scientific communication and for this, he has distinguished himself from others.

Once again, the key is differentiation: to stay etched in people's minds you have to be different from the average of what they see by scrolling the Instagram feed.

You have to find your way and you can do it only by attempts, making mistakes, and trying again, there is no recipe for the perfect video. The only recipe I know, because I tried it first, is to observe what others are doing, those that are already well-positioned, and adapt it to your style, to your way of speaking, to what you want to communicate.

Try, fail, and try again (and don't forget about mistakes).

This was until the advent of IGTV, the Instagram TV, because with Instagram TV things have changed and, from my point of view, for the better.

I take a step back. When Zuckerberg and associates launched Instagram TV in June 2018, many argued that it would not work because "imagine who watches TV on Instagram."

A billion people, potentially, in every part of the world.

Obviously, IGTV was not a flop, also thanks to the investments and strategies developed to launch it. Starting with the ability to publish previews of recorded videos for TV on your feed.

The revolution that IGTV has brought to social media begins with the duration and format of the clips which, in addition to the 'usual' vertical, today include the horizontal, so if you want to see a video on your mobile, you turn it and watch it comfortably. There is also an important update from the duration side: the clips (which must not weigh more than 3.6 GB with a maximum resolution of 4K) can be up to 10 minutes long.

The trend of Instagram is to allow, in the future, to publish videos of unlimited duration, as on YouTube.

In my opinion, but above all looking at the data on the views of my video content before and after IGTV, it is a huge opportunity to gain visibility and new followers.

Comparing the numbers of people who have watched some of my Instagram clips, I saw that if I could have done an average of 30,000 before, since IGTV I have reached an average of three times that, with peaks of 180,000 views.

My advice? Try Instagram TV, make videos, and upload them directly there, also because you have the option of publishing a one-minute preview on your feed.

Here's what to do:

- Record your video (in vertical format as mentioned);
- Edit it, even using an easy App like InShot; once you have selected the video you want to edit, you have a whole series of tools that will allow you to cut it, to increase or reduce the part of the video that can be displayed, to cut it to take only the sections that interest you, to add some text (my advice is to always do it, using a few words, positioned on two bands, one above and one below the clip, which summarize the topic you are talking about in the video), and finally save it on the phone;
- Upload it to IGTV giving it a title and, at the same time, select the one-minute preview to publish on your feed.

The preview is essential because it is a bit like a trailer of your video. People watch it and, if the content interests them, they will click on the IGTV icon to continue watching it.

When you doubt whether or not videos can work on Instagram, consider this: the investment policies of Zuck & Co. have moved on two fronts: business (the possibility of selling products and services directly from social profiles, without having to browse them) and videos.

To Sum Up

When you decide to upload a video remember that:

- The ideal format for the Instagram feed is 1:1 (the square), bundled (with bands at the top and/or bottom) with explanatory writings;
- On IGTV the ideal format is horizontal, you can record and publish videos up to 10 minutes long.

How to Create Your Own Video for Instagram Using Only Your Mobile?

To start posting your videos you can use a simple and free app like InShot.

With this app (but also with others, equally free) you can:

- Record the video;
- Upload it to the app;

- Put it in the ideal format (1:1 square which automatically gives you the top band and the bottom band);
- Add the text you prefer, choosing among different fonts;
- Add cover images that you may already have on your phone (and also icons);
- Export it in the best, most qualitative format.

4.6 Instagram Stories

Instagram Stories are 15-second videos that you can use to maintain a direct relationship with the people who follow you. When you open Instagram, you will find them at the top, they are those circles with profile photos that open with a touch. Slowly they are supplanting photos (again for the reason I told you just now for which the direction taken from Menlo Park is to push video and business on this social network).

There are characters like Jay-Z, and his wife Beyonce, who daily post dozens of Stories and only a couple of photos, so does his wife and like Victoria Beckham and many others. The Stories have basically been cloned from Snapchat and, probably, have been designed precisely to involve a young audience.

That said, today everyone uses them, or almost everyone.

The characteristic of this function is its provisional nature, let me explain: the videos or photos that are posted on Stories have a limited duration in time; 24 hours later they are deleted unless you decide to save them using Story Saver (for Android) or StoryRepost (for iPhone). In any case, keep in mind that they can be a good test to see which content works and engages your followers the most and which doesn't.

From the first moment they appeared, the Stories could be modified with stickers, animated and written GIFs that made them customizable and original, but today you can increase the involvement of people using surveys: basically, these are still two stickers that allow you to ask a question (of any kind) to the people who follow you giving two answer options.

For example, you might ask: "Do you prefer me to make a video on the mating of penguins, or one on how their burrows are made?"

In the two buttons enter the two options and, at the end of the 24 hours of the life of the story, you will see not only the number of views you have obtained but also the percentage of the vote.

In this way you have achieved a double result: you have involved those who follow you in a decision-making process and you have discovered what interests your audience most.

In any case, whatever your strategy, you should think about its originality.

4.7 How to Understand If a Content Works on Instagram

Basically, there is a way to tell if your content, video, or photo, works.

It is a question of assigning a grade from 1 to 10 to these 4 questions:

1. How important is what you are publishing to your audience, i.e., how much value does that image have for those who follow you?
2. How impossible and how rare is it to find that content?
3. How much is reproducible by the average of the people who follow you? That is, how easy is it for your follower to take a photo or a video like yours?
4. How irreplaceable is it as an interest, as an entertainment? That is, how much is preferable for

those who follow you to watch what you have posted rather than an episode of a streaming series?

In other words: let's say you take a picture of yourself in front of a swimming pool and answer these 4 questions:

- How important is what you are posting to your audience? Well, suppose you have an audience of people who are very interested in swimming pools, then on the first question, you can assign 10 as a score.

- How rare is it to find a photo of someone in front of a swimming pool? I would say there are 7 billion, so the value, in this case, is 1.

- How much is reproducible from the average of the people who follow you? It doesn't take long to take a picture in front of a swimming pool, again 1.

- How irreplaceable is it as entertainment? Maybe yours is a cute photo and someone would rather look at it than watching 50 minutes of Game of Thrones. In this case, the grade is 2.

Once all the questions have been scored, we proceed with the sum: 10 + 1 + 1 + 2 = 14. We divide the sum by 4 (remembering that the maximum is, of course, 40) and we have the result, specifically just over 3. Moral, the photo in the pool does not work much.

4.8 The Ideal Amount of Instagram Content and How to Make It by Yourself or with a Professional

Today, if one has a serious strategy, he ideally posts 4 contents a day: for example two in the morning and two in the afternoon/evening (also based on the times when his followers are most present on Instagram) and 5 Stories a day.

Assuming that it is not easy for everyone to post with so much regularity and frequency, and also assuming that if we want to put down a serious and effective strategy we must not deviate much from this amount of content, it does not mean that we have to do everything alone.

If, for example, you do not have time to dedicate yourself every day to making videos and Stories, you can choose to get help from a video maker who, with a fixed frequency (once a month, every two weeks, or every 10 days), records you in the course of a day, while doing something interesting for your audience (attending an event, training, meeting someone), edit the material produced and send it to your mobile phone ready to be published.

This way you can optimize your presence on Instagram because the point is that you don't necessarily have to produce content every day to be present every day on Instagram.

4.9 What to Post on Instagram? Some Practical Examples

Premise: at the base of all your strategies, don't forget that there is always positioning: what is the story you are telling on Instagram?

What's the video I'm coming to see on your feed?

Does it have twists and an engaging storyline or is it agonizing boredom?

If in doubt, remember the 4 questions with which you can assign a score to your production.

That said, it's important to test, and basically mix, post types (video/text/images but also product/News/contest/etc.).

At this point, here are some practical examples of what to post on Instagram so as not to make your followers die of boredom.

A. Original/Creative/Funny/Particular Uses of Your Product/Service

If you have, for example, a bags shop, instead of posting a photo of your beautiful handbag, you might try to think about what uses of the bag might be interesting for your customers.

If the bag is famous for the resistance of its materials, you could take a series of photos in the most extreme environments.

If it's the quality that makes that bag an exceptional product, you could document all the steps required to make it.

If the design is the strong point, well, you know it.

B. Your Customer

Why tell the story of your services when your client can?

Are you a lawyer? Instead of explaining to those who follow you why you are very good, telling them that they have to come to your studio, you could collect short interviews with your clients about the results they have achieved since you have helped them.

If you are a tattoo artist, you can think of images of your clients just tattooed by you, etc.

C. Award and Celebration

It's never the best to talk about you, but if you've just won the Oscars, well let me know.

Or if you have won the award for the best dental practice in Las Vegas for the third year in a row, again, you can say it.

Special awards and celebrations always have their appeal if posted in the right way.

D. Popular Hashtags

I'm not a fan of hashtags, not at all, but sometimes you have mass and custom phenomena that are collected under one or more specific hashtags that you can hook to present your point of view.

E. Latest News

Are you a great hairstylist? Then post a video of yours commenting on how you would style Trump!

Current events always have a thousand ideas to never run out of ideas.

F. Behind the Scenes

What happens behind the scenes in your

company/studio/shop/laboratory/office?

If you think about the behind-the-scenes of a lot of famous movies and the curiosity they arouse, you understand that you too can produce content that may interest your audience on Instagram.

Maybe you have a fish restaurant and you can show when you go to the market at 4 in the morning to choose the freshest one. What method do you use to choose it?

How do you know if it's good or not?

Unveil yours behind the scenes.

G. Practical Advice

Do you have a t-shirt e-commerce?

Show us which shirt to use for each occasion.

What are the best color combinations, which shirt goes best on each dress?

H. Ask

I don't have all the answers, what about you?

Don't be afraid to ask your audience.

Suggestions, preferences, advice, indications, etc.

Between the Stories' surveys and the open questions in the feed, you have a wide variety of options.

I. Time Machine

How were you 10 years ago?

What about your product 20 years ago?

And how has the market changed?

The "nostalgia" posts help to give the context of the evolution of your work and of your customers.

4.10 Exercise to Do Right Away

At this point you have all the elements you need to develop your strategy which, remember, should have these requirements to work:

- Be original;
- Be consistent with the goal you have set yourself;
- Post with a certain frequency (my suggestion is at least 1 new content per day);
- Provide many videos and many Stories (you also need

the latter to increase the level of involvement of your audience);

- Make the most of the opportunity offered by IGTV (on which Instagram is investing a lot);

- Do not be blatantly marketing (i.e., if your goal is to sell brushes, you can also make videos in which you explain how to preserve the softness of your hair using a thousand tricks and your brush);

- It must be yours, capable of identifying you as a company or character.

So, if so far we have said that it is important to draw inspiration from the strongest, now it is the time to apply what you felt worked in the profiles you followed.

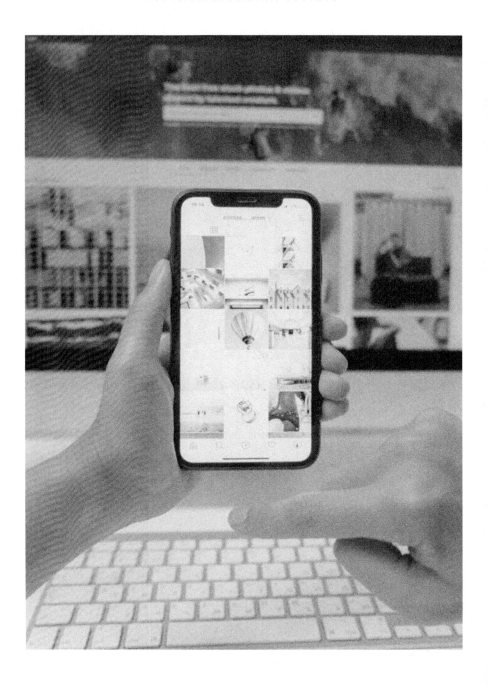

Chapter 5
An Eye on Quality

When we talk about design and visual communication, a very small premise is required. Many underestimate its value, thinking it is a purely "aesthetic" issue.

Nothing could be more wrong. The images present and represent us or our brand. It's marketing to all intents and purposes.

The following are practical tips for those without skills. Just be aware that there are no "rigid" rules. The beauty of this sector is breaking the mold, although in this case, I would suggest you do it with the advice of a professional or a communication agency.

Their personalized analysis will evaluate the opportunity to remodel some concepts. Before proceeding, a question you should ask yourself is: do you want to make posts that are only beautiful or above all that work?

If you are here, you are certainly not someone with lower standards.

5.1 Filters in Abundance

One of the most common mistakes, before posting images and photos, is to select Instagram filters without any criteria.

The practical advice, therefore, is to "become attached" to a single filter and try to keep it over time in all the images of the posts.

This will allow you to increase the perception of your visual identity, especially when the user finds himself in front of your profile screen.

A profile that uses filters that change to the same shades is more effective than the others.

Obviously, the situation is different for those who by profession are for example a designer/photographer/artist and therefore need to differentiate the images because that is the true value he is offering to his public.

Indeed, in these cases, the advice is not to use any filter. In this way, you will give greater authenticity and therefore value to your contents.

5.2 Do You Have a Nice Personality?

The text is design. Let's start from this assumption and we will get along well. And, as we have already seen, design is marketing.

If it is true that an image communicates more than a thousand words, it is equally true that, with well-integrated text, it increases the effectiveness of the entire message.

Please, be careful not to overdo the text. It may not be well seen by the algorithm and therefore partially penalize your reach.

From a practical point of view, adding text to an image is absolutely not complicated.

But, if you are totally new to design and layout, do not worry.

These apps help you by offering you several already well-structured templates, which will allow you to produce material very quickly. Be it photos or even videos.

If, on the other hand, you are a DIY lover, here are some quick and practical tips to avoid the most common mistakes when using text on an image:

1. Choose a single style of character/font that can

communicate and accompany you in your sector of reference.

I won't bore you with endless lists of font types. Broadly speaking we could try to divide them into simpler and more intuitive categories such as "rigid," "soft," "elegant," and "playful."

It's up to you to select the most appropriate one, trying to stay consistent with your sector.

For example, avoid using a "playful" font if you have a company that deals with business and finance or if you are a lawyer.

2. Select a single font for all your posts. This will also help create a stronger visual identity for your brand.
3. Never use Comic Sans.

5.3 Which Is Your Favorite Color?

Let's start with a question right away.

If you think of red, what is the first thing that comes to your mind?

Love? Passion? Danger? Alarm?

As you can see, all the potential answers are correct. Indeed, any color can communicate different feelings and emotions based on the context in which it is used.

However, I will bring you below, in broad outline, a brief guide on the main meaning, more important than the main colors:

- **RED:** love, danger, passion, strength, anger, stop;

- **BLUE:** trust, relaxation, intelligence, professionalism, reliability;

- **GREEN:** nature, growth, freshness, tranquility, envy, hope, green light;

- **YELLOW:** optimism, energy, attention, warmth, wisdom;

- **ORANGE:** friendship, happiness, health, good mood, balance;

- **BLACK:** elegance, wealth, strength, evil;

- **WHITE:** light, purity, simplicity;

- **PURPLE:** mystery, future, mourning, spirituality, luxury, magic;

Therefore, I recommend always pay close attention to the context and to the images/symbols that match the colors.

5.4 But How Many Do You Imagine?

Square, horizontal, vertical, slide-carousel.

Each image format/size, in addition to being a valid method for alternating the proposal of contents, can, if used creatively, contribute to the construction of a "well-designed" profile.

On the other hand, the slide layout, also called carousel, deserves a few more words. Usually used in a "standard" way or as a simple multi-photo.

The practical advice, to make it more attractive, is to use it creatively and unconventionally.

How? A single image is perfectly cut into consecutive squares which, when the slide is scrolled, allows you to show the hidden part of the photo that will be perfectly attached to the previous one.

To create the most "creative" posts like those above, there is obviously professional software such as Adobe Photoshop, but also very simple and intuitive free applications that you will easily find in your store.

5.5 Can I Tell You a Story?

Often the Instagram Stories are simply photos or "shares" of posts from the feed. If you want to try to stand out from the crowd, you could create vertical layouts already conceived and designed in a story dimension.

Also, in this case, Adobe Spark, with its templates/models, proposes the Instagram Stories format.

In this way, through the visual communication within the Stories, you will increase the value and perception of your brand identity.

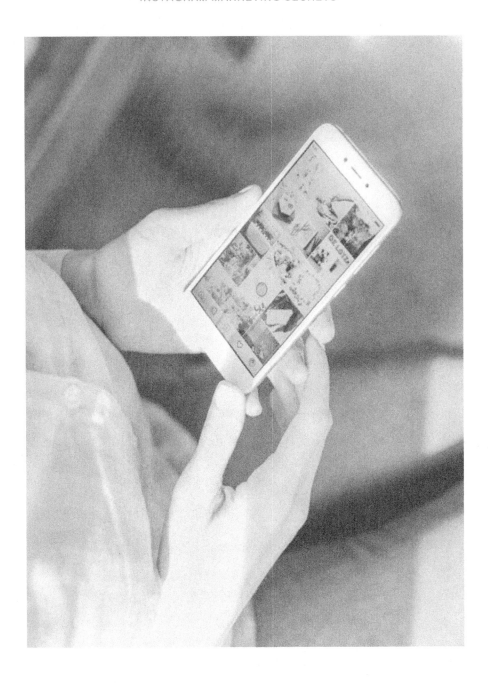

Chapter 6
Promoting Your Profile

Yes, you might have the most stratospheric profile in the world, but if you don't decide to promote it a lot, you will hardly reach the goal of having a numerically consistent audience willing to buy your products (or services) or to follow you consistently recognizing you as 'the penguin expert' or anything else.

In other words, if you do not also take into account the promotion activities of your content, Instagram alone will not be able to make you reach all the audience that could be really interested in you, what you do, and what you say.

So, in addition to a content strategy, you also need to include a promotional one. In this chapter, I will tell you what, in my experience, works best.

As always, this does not mean that there are no other possibilities and that they can be just as good: the difference lies in the fact that I have experimented on myself with the ideas I am about to give you and they have given me satisfactory results.

6.1 How to Promote Your Content

You have many ways to make your content known on Instagram: the most immediate, the one that immediately comes to mind is to establish a budget to promote what you publish; Instagram ADV, and later in this chapter I'll talk about it at length.

As far as I have been able to verify, whatever type of promo you want to adopt, I do not think you can do without a budget to invest in your social profile: if you don't, if you think you can give up this aspect, it will be difficult for you to get out of a very narrow niche of audience.

If, on the one hand, it is true that it is not necessary to have "a thousand million" followers to have a profile that works, it is also true that once you have established the target of people you want to address you must use every means you have to achieve it.

However, given this premise, which is essential for you to increase your fanbase to be 'credible and attractive,' you can begin to think that "if you go faster alone, you go further together."

What does it mean? It means that, once you have given your profile a bit of mass, you can start looking around and start collaborations with the influencers that are most similar to you, in an exchange that is favorable to you and them.

6.2 Instagram Advertising

There is for Instagram, as well as for Facebook, the possibility of promoting paid content and I advise you to use it to ensure that. Through a targeted audience, you can reach an increasing number of people who are really interested in you, to your product or service.

In general, 'advertising' on this, as on other social networks, allows you to increase the awareness of a brand and can be functional in bringing visibility to a Web page.

To proceed with the Instagram ADV, you can use the Ads Manager (from which you also manage Facebook ads, but be careful to keep campaigns well separated).

The first step to keep in mind when investing in ADV is targeting the audience you intend to send the message to: you can also proceed using the same type of audience that you have selected for other FB campaigns, diverting it to Instagram or creating a completely new target.

When choosing the composition of the audience, you can rely

on several factors such as age, place of birth, gender, and common interests.

Next, you need to understand what the purpose of the content (video or photo) you want to promote is. Generally, the focus is on promoting the brand, i.e., creating content to be sponsored to show it to as many people as possible who, according to the targeting, may be interested in purchasing its products or services.

Another possible goal is that of coverage, which allows you to maximize the number of people who see your ad.So you can decide to sponsor content by linking it to your website (personal or business) or, again, to increase your followers, i.e., people who follow your profile.

Consider sponsoring your Stories too, Instagram allows it and we have seen that these are a great way to create closeness and arouse the interactions of the people who follow you.

Considering that we are talking about ADV, and therefore about the money you use to push your content, I advise you to be as careful as possible to a couple of factors: the quality of your message (which should be particularly accurate and captivating) and the target of the people to whom you address it.

If you miss this last step, the risk is not to achieve a satisfactory result concerning the investment you have made.

Finally, to better position your content, you can use hashtags that, even more than normal posts, will help you capture the attention of the audience that may be interested in what you propose.

6.3 Types of ADV on Instagram and Examples from Which You Can Take Inspiration

Let's move on to practice with a few examples from which you can draw inspiration for your profile.

Photo Ads

1. **Simple and Strong Image that Captures Attention**

It works because it is fun but at the same time targeted if you offer a dog-washing service.

2. **Evocative Image**

In this case, we see an image that promotes a dance school.

It works because it is perfect for Instagram, and you want to share it since it is a mix of art and optical illusion.

3. Nice Image

If you are in the world of catering, food, or related fields, consider something that has a message, food.

Video Ads

1. Simple and Immediate Video

The video in this case shows the advantage of using a Ring doorbell (it works because in 5 seconds you understand the company's value proposition).

2. Effect Video

If you want to focus on the charm of the extreme and of the challenge, Under Armor is for you.

3. A Video Is Worth More Than 1000 Words

Do you have a cool product? Show it. Don't describe it, show it.

Stories Ads

1. In addition to the most complex creativity you can imagine making your Stories, you can also use simpler techniques such as quick assembly of several images in a single story.

2. However, you can also choose a static image that relies on convenience.

To Sum Up

To promote your Instagram content, keep these tips in mind:

- Target your audience well based on what you promote. Remember that you use the Facebook Ads Manager and, probably, part of your audience you have already selected previously and you simply have to redirect it to Instagram;

- When targeting the public keep in mind factors such as age, gender, interests, geolocation, etc.

- Focus on the goal you want to achieve: do you promote a brand? A product? Yourself?

- You can sponsor content by linking it to your website (personal or corporate) and inserting the link that opens it directly;

- You can sponsor both photos and videos and Stories;

- Use hashtags to better position your content and get it to really interested people.

6.4 Partnering with Influencers

At this point you have your profile, you are filling it with content, you have invested in ADV campaigns, and you are starting to obtain results that you consider satisfactory: people follow you, comment, and interact with you.

But that's still not enough.

No, because you have another option that I recommend you use: collaborating with influencers who are similar to you (for what they communicate, for how they do it).

It is clear that if you have 12,000 followers and the person (or company) you want to contact has 4 million, you must ensure that your content, especially the one in which you would like to involve them, also benefits them.

But how can you, with your 12,000 followers, represent a 'good investment' for those who already have a lot of visibility? As usual, you can only do this by using all the features that make a video (for IGTV or Instagram) a good product.

Among the possible options for contacting an influencer, I advise you not to underestimate the interviews.

You can get involved to reach the person you are interested in:

- Try to find a common point with her/him: for example, I play tennis and Will Smith is passionate about tennis. That is something I could use to get in touch with him;

- If the character you are interested in is busy promoting a product of his (for example, Obama is on tour in Colorado to promote his latest book), this is the right time to try and ask him for an interview;

- If the character you want to reach is too well known for you, you can start by interviewing the people who are close to him: like Obama's personal trainer, his bodyguard, etc. In this way, you create an aura of credibility among the people he is in contact with so that when you try to ask him to give you an interview you are no longer a complete stranger but someone his friends can put in a good word for.

People love to talk about themselves, especially men and women from the business world, as CEOs or managers, so trying to approach them by asking for an interview is also a good way to carry on and introduce your business to these potential customers in an elegant way.

To contact an influencer, you can send him a ping on Instagram and, when he replies, start a dialogue with her/him by presenting your project, explaining who you are and what you do, and how you would like to involve her/him.

The relationship must be a 'win-win,' otherwise, your collaboration proposal would be a bit scrounging and for those who already have an audience, it would have no appeal.

I do not recommend the use of tags towards someone who has "a hundred thousand" followers and who, inevitably, will not notice you or, in the worst-case scenario, could be bothered by the aggressiveness of a tag placed on content that does not belong to them.

A tool you can use to find partners is Mention, which allows you to find out which content and profiles generate the most interactions.

To Sum Up

Produce quality content, invest in ADV so that your audience is always greater, and involve influencers by presenting them with a collaboration proposal for specific content. And when you get it, remember to put some budget on that video in which you chat with Will Smith or Obama.

The Curious Case of Daniel Wellington (and His Successful Strategy)

Among the paradigmatic case histories on how to best use collaborations with influencers, one, in particular, is worth remembering for its originality: that of Daniel Wellington watches.

Basically, the company decided to promote its watches using mini and micro-influencers (from 2000 to 10,000 followers) to whom it gave a watch in exchange for a photo (in a perfect win-win logic) made according to common and pre-established guidelines but leaving everyone the freedom to express their creativity in the photo.

The result was always different with pleasant images and, to date, with a fanbase of 4.9 million followers.

6.5 But How Do I Contact an Influencer?

Everyone can write to an influencer, but not everyone has the same chance of being taken into consideration by the influencer they wrote to.

For this reason, below, you will find the basic rules that I recommend you follow to have a greater number of chances of really getting in touch with the character you sent your message to:

1. Do not forget that the influencer often asks himself this question: what is the advantage I derive from this collaboration, what benefits does it bring?

2. Be concise and brief, indeed very short, you will have a greater chance that the influencer will reach the bottom of your message and not leave it halfway;

3. Don't ask, offer; every day an influencer has someone who wants something. Claims, requests, emergencies, and urgent appeals to save humanity. Don't be on the list of those who break up to have something, put yourself on the list of those who represent an advantage, help, support, and an extra value;

4. You are not the phenomenon: do not make the mistake of writing to a well-known character as if you were Ronaldo. If you are Ronaldo, then you don't need to write to anyone.

If you are Ronaldo, people will look for you! The most hateful thing you can do is write to the person with whom you are coming in contact by putting them in a hurry, pushing on the urgency, and fearing unique and unrepeatable opportunities (remember an influencer does not need you, you are the one who needs him. Always think about what you can do for him not him for you).

Now that we have the ground rules, here are some examples of texts you can use:

- **Preview** (offer preview access to something)

Hello "Influencer Name,"

My name is xxxxx and I realize yyyy.

We are about to release a tool that allows you to make what's beautiful even more beautiful, if you are interested, this is the link for you in preview.

- **Business offer** (if you have a budget, offer an opportunity to do business together)

Hello "Influencer Name,"

My name is xxxxx and I realize yyyy.

I have been following your content for xxxx years and I appreciate your work in the zzzzzz industry.

We would like to work with you to let your audience know

about our xxxx product which we think is very similar and very useful for all your fans.

Can we have contact with those who follow your partnerships so as to deepen methods and economics?

- **Research** (only if you have a research with really new, original, and interesting data)

Hello "Influencer Name,"

My name is xxxxx and I realize yyyy.

I'm bothering you because we just published research on 2,000 basketball players and their IQ. The results are truly amazing and by following you we think it might be of your interest.

- **Let's talk about you** (even influencers have an ego, often very big)

If you have written an article or made a video about one of them, why not report it to the person concerned? As usual, it must be something genuine and well done!

Hello "Influencer Name,"

My name is xxxxx and I realize yyyy.

We have just published a video that analyzes the best pizza makers on the web and we included you.

We tried to analyze the 72 techniques that make your pizza so good.

Let us know if we got it!

- **Interview** (if you want to interview someone)

Subject: Interview to promote your new book/movie/YOU/... on my xxxx followers

Hello "Influencer Name!"

I would like to interview you to promote the video on my community of xxxx followers.

For the past few years, I have interviewed from xxxx to yyyy and have specialized in the field of zzzzz for xxxx years.

Here is an example of a video I made with xxxx link.

6.6 "Bot" No Thanks

Let's repeat together, the Bots are mean and we don't use them.

Really, guys, Bots are not ethical, they are a 'rip off' because they don't really represent you, your ideas, your tastes, your opinions.

They are a bluff that someone (many actually) uses to keep their audience and try to increase it by giving the illusion of participation and interest that are not really real.

Bots are artificial intelligence that basically replaces people and deceive users who believe they have received a like from someone who actually did nothing, didn't interact with them, just set up a bot to act in its place.

Instagram, we said it immediately, is a clean social network where even the Bots do not have an easy life. It is so very clean, I mean that it gave birth to the practice of Shadowban which, for some time, drastically reduces the audience to which the contents of the profile are shown (usually it is business profiles) even if it is sponsored content if you are caught using Bots.

Personally, I agree with Instagram's policy which, in this way, tries to remain a clean place where reality, albeit filtered and perhaps even embellished, is essentially what you see.

6.7 Exercise to Do Right Away

Remembering that promoting yourself will always cost you less than being swept away by the competition, now it's time to take action so:

- Identify the audience that your content might be interested in (take into account age, gender, place where it is, interests, etc.);
- Produce ad hoc content for your audience;
- Establish a budget to invest in ADV Instagram;
- Monitor the results of your campaigns to understand if they work (for content and targeting) and if necessary, adjust the shot;
- Identify potential partners with whom to create synergy and share useful content for both.

Conclusion

At this point, you are ready to create an Instagram account that rocks and this is the lineup that will help you do it:

1. Establish your goals based on who you are, what your characteristics and aspirations are.

2. Identify your audience and create your buyer persona (your typical customer).

3. Followers are not everything: the success of your Instagram account does not depend solely on the number of people who follow you, but on the real interest they have in what you propose to them.

4. Study the strategies of influencers who target the people you want to reach yourself and replicate them in your own style.

5. Create your account:

   - Write your bio specifying who you are and what you do;

   - Put a link to your site or to a product/service you want to promote;

   - Choose a professional but not fake photo (you can also use objects: if you are a footballer, a ball; if you are a make-up artist, a palette!).

6. Produce quality content that will interest your audience:

- When you publish a video, remember that the ideal format for the Instagram feed is the square (1:1) with the bands above and below that you can fill with text, so that it immediately captures the attention of those who see it.

   For IGTV the ideal format is horizontal, and videos can be up to 10 minutes long.

   You record Stories, the 15-second videos that disappear in 24 hours, vertically;

- The ideal amount of content for a serious strategy is 4 per day (two in the morning and two in the afternoon/evening, depending on when your audience is most present) plus 5 Stories;

- If you do not have time to record and publish videos every day, contact a video maker and set one day a month, or every two weeks, in which to be followed and filmed, then entrust him with the editing of your videos according to your needs;

- If you want to produce your videos by yourself, download an app like OneShot that in a few minutes allows you to create quality editing in the most suitable format;

- Do not forget the 4 key points to understand if your content is of quality (How important is what you are publishing for your audience? How rare is it to find it? How much is it reproducible by the average of the people who follow you? How irreplaceable as entertainment?). Give each of these points a score from 1 to 10: the higher it is, the higher the quality of your content.

7. Promote your content using Instagram ADV:
    - Set the goal of your promo: do you want to have more followers? Promote your brand? Push a product?
    - Target your audience based on your goal (remember the buyer persona);
    - Use hashtags to better position your promo and be found by the right people.

8. Contact influencers by proposing a collaboration that is beneficial to both of you. To get in touch with them you can find a passion or a common interest and leverage this:
    - Interviews are a good way to make yourself known and build beneficial collaborations for you and the influencer you want to reach;
    - If the characters you want to contact are 'too

famous,' start by interviewing the people around them who, at the decisive moment, will be able to put in a good word for you.

9. Do not use BOTs: Instagram is a clean social network, that is, it rewards real interaction between people.

10. Experiment, try and try again, get it wrong quickly and quickly build your strategy.

Useful Tools

Before leaving, I would like to point out these links from which you can access a series of useful tools for an Instagram account that rocks:

https://storrito.com/

(It allows not only post scheduling but also Stories scheduling management.)

https://onlypult.com

(Platform for scheduling posts on Instagram and other major social networks, plus statistical analysis of performance.)

https://skillpost.me/

(Multi-account tool with which to schedule the publication of posts.)

https://hootsuite.com/instagram

(Among the various things that can be done with the tool, there is programming and post-management for the Instagram platform.)

https://later.com/

(A set of tools for managing your Instagram account, including an editorial calendar, a tab in which to check the preview of your feed before publishing, a tool for managing scheduled posts, and one to identify the content posted by users and make a repost. In the business plans, there is the link in the bio function that allows you to make clickable content in the feed to bring traffic to landing pages and products.)

https://planable.io/

(Collaborative platform to schedule posts on Twitter, Facebook, and Instagram. It has a visual dashboard where comments on posts are also shown, and you can check how your content would look in the feed before publishing it.)

https://preppr.com/

(Tool for publishing scheduled posts via the platform and app. The app is currently only available for ¡OS.)

Analysis

https://hypeauditor.com/

(Tool to check an Instagram audience, to identify accounts with fake followers. Through an AI system, the tool can tell the gender, average age, interests of the public, and identify an estimated cash value for each post of an account: useful for those who want to analyze their audience or that of a profile with which they want to collaborate.)

https://hypeauditor.com/top-instagram/

(Hyperauditor tool that allows you to see the profiles of the top 1000 Instagram influencers divided by category).

http://www.primeforinstagram.com/

(¡OS app with which you can analyze the performance of posts and understand what is the best time to publish new content.)

https://buzzweb.pro/

(Allows audience analysis, inspecting followers, and is able to divide real ones from fake accounts and give a value to a potential influencer account.)

https://www.socialinsider.io/instagram-analytics

(A comparative dashboard with historical data from you and your competitors, which allows you to understand what is doing well with your strategy and what you should change. Among other things, it allows you to analyze the performance of the hashtags used.)

https://www.trywefind.com/

(A Chrome plugin that gives you statistical data on public Instagram accounts. It tells you the average number of posts published in a week, average engagement, and the number of likes and comments on posts.)

Hashtags

https://itunes.apple.com/us/app/hashtag-expert-for-ig/id1256222789

(iOS app for identifying the right hashtags for a given content.)

https://keywordtool.io/instagram

(A platform where, among other things, you can enter a keyword in a certain language and discover all the hashtags related to that term on Instagram.)

https://play.google.com/store/apps/details?id=com.kimcy929.hashtags&hl=it

(HashTags for Instagram is an Android app to discover the most used hashtags divided by topic/category.)

https://flick.tech/

(Flick helps entrepreneurs, content creators and small businesses reach their target audience organically by searching and analyzing the most used hashtags.)

https://play.google.com/store/apps/details?id=com.upcurve.magnify

(Magnify is an Android app to automatically apply the most suitable hashtags for a given content. Just open the app, add the caption and the subject of the post to have all the hashtags automatically inserted in the shot.)

https://instashow.tv/

(Tool with which to create a slideshow with images that contain a certain hashtag. Useful for example during an event, to show live images with the same hashtag, shared by multiple users.)

Graphics
https://www.kapwing.com/instagram-story-templates

(A series of templates to be used to create Stories with captivating graphics. You can use images, text, and videos.)

https://postmuseapp.com/

(iOS and Android app to create Stories made of photo collages plus texts with particular fonts.)

Lisa—Smart Photo Assistant

(iOS and Android, it helps you predict which photo will have the greatest impact on your audience thanks to a machine learning system. Access your photo gallery, select some photos to compare them, choose the right hashtags, and post.)

https://yttoig.com/

(A platform where you can post your YouTube videos on Instagram.)

https://itunes.apple.com/us/app/splitstory-for-instagram-video/id1443189644

(Cut Story Long Video Splitter is a ¡OS app for cutting long videos into 15-second pieces for your Instagram Stories.)

https://itunes.apple.com/us/app/quoth-quotes-and-memes/id1445458619

(Quoth is a ¡OS app that allows you to combine the best phrases of celebrities with your photos.)

https://play.google.com/store/apps/details?id=fmy.latian.storysplit&hl=it

(Android app to cut long videos into 15-second chunks, suitable for your Instagram Stories.)

https://getuplet.com/

(A software with which to upload photos to Instagram directly from your Mac, adjusting the aspect ratio without losing the quality of the shot.)

https://www.canva.com/

(Simple creation of graphics, with different formats including those suitable for Instagram content.)

Gif Me

(¡OS and Android app to quickly create animated Gifs for Instagram).

https://spark.adobe.com/it-IT/

(App with which to create captivating graphics, with images and photos.)

https://www.storyzapp.com/

(Create animated Stories starting from a static photo. You have a series of filters to use on images, with which to give movement to a part of an image, leaving everything else fixed.)

Other

https://rewindapp.co/

(¡OS and Android app to find and review old posts published on your Instagram.)

https://buffer.com/shop-grid

(Platform that allows you to create a landing page with all the products you advertise on Instagram, putting the link in bio.)

https://voicestory.app/

(It is a ¡OS app completely different from the others, which allows you to bring your voice into Instagram Stories. Just use the app to record your voice, edit the transcript that is automatically created by the app, and publish.)

https://twis.io/

(A platform with which you can choose the winner among who comments or interacts with your post. Automatically remove repeating accounts.)

https://filtergram.app/

(A website where you can create your own Instagram feed, made up of only a few accounts, without commercial interruptions or distractions.)

https://www.zine.so/

(You can turn your Instagram account into a visual website containing all the images in your account.)

https://widget.fastory.io/

(Free widget that allows you to bring the Stories of an Instagram account to the website.)

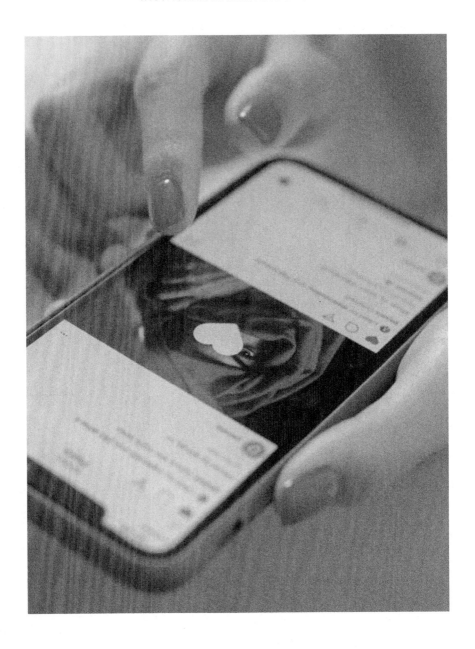

Printed in Great Britain
by Amazon